T0209130

The Short Dance

A Journey of Life, Death, and Beyond

Leonidas Kolokathis

BALBOA.
PRESS
A DIVISION OF HAY HOUSE

Balboa Press books may be ordered through booksellers or by contacting:

Balboa Press
A Division of Hay House
1663 Liberty Drive
Bloomington, IN 47403
www.balboapress.com.au
1 (877) 407-4847

Because of the dynamic nature of the Internet, any web addresses or links contained in this book may have changed since publication and may no longer be valid. The views expressed in this work are solely those of the author and do not necessarily reflect the views of the publisher, and the publisher hereby disclaims any responsibility for them.

The author of this book does not dispense medical advice or prescribe the use of any technique as a form of treatment for physical, emotional, or medical problems without the advice of a physician, either directly or indirectly. The intent of the author is only to offer information of a general nature to help you in your quest for emotional and spiritual well-being. In the event you use any of the information in this book for yourself, which is your constitutional right, the author and the publisher assume no responsibility for your actions.

Any people depicted in stock imagery provided by Thinkstock are models, and such images are being used for illustrative purposes only.
Certain stock imagery © Thinkstock.

Print information available on the last page.

ISBN: 978-1-5043-0309-5 (sc)
ISBN: 978-1-5043-0310-1 (e)

Balboa Press rev. date: 07/05/2016

Geraldine, you touched my life, you gave me love's true embrace, you taught me strength and you showed me peace. You left too soon yet at exactly the right time. I will never forget what you have given me. All things considered, I am the most blessed to have had your love and embrace. Geraldine this book is for you. Thank you for all you have taught me and for all that I am. I trust you will be looking down proud of who I am.

Leonidas

The following pages contain quotes, ones which I have collected over time. Some I have come up with on my own and others are thoughts from my children when asked about their mum. They all mean much to me; when I heard them they struck a chord deep in my soul and I felt the need to write them down. The ones that are from me, well, those are odd as I am not certain where they have come from; some just are random thoughts of reflection. Some well... They are from Spirit....

"Sometimes Life gives you the bitterest of pills to swallow. Those brave enough to swallow it shall receive the reward, those who spit it out will have it presented to them again at a later time."

Leonidas

"The Path To Paradise Begins in Hell"

Dante

"In the middle of the journey of my life I came to myself within a dark wood where the straight way was lost

Dante

It is not the years in your life yet the life in your years

Geordie Kolokathis

I love you always

Daynon Kolokathis

The Person Who is Always There

You breathe your first breath
You take your first step
You say your first word
I will always be there

Your very first birthday
Your very first Christmas
Your first ever day of school
I am still there

Your first job
Your magical white wedding
The birth of your child
I am there

Your last job
Your last breath
An emotional funeral
I am now with you again

Caitlin Kolokathis

"Life is in the future not in the past, to embrace the future you embrace life, to embrace the past you embrace death"
Wizard's rule from the Sword of truth series

Terry Goodkind.

"Your life is your own – do with it what you please"
Wizard's Rule from Sword of truth series

Terry Goodkind.

I sometimes think and wonder, wonder and think and I
find that all these thoughts come in to your head like:
Why is it in your biggest moments of grief
you find the most amazing strength?
Why is it when you dip in to your deepest despair you
find your true self? Why is it in your moments of true
ecstasy you find where you should be travelling?

And why is it when you sit with your own true self
you see things you don't like and only when you
accept them can you become who you must???

Leonidas

IN ORDER TO HEAR ALL YOU MUST DO IS LISTEN!
IN ORDER TO SEE ALL YOU NEED TO DO IS LOOK!
IN ORDER TO SENSE ALL YOU NEED TO DO IS FEEL!
IF YOU WANT THEM TO HEAR
YOU HAVE TO BUT TALK!
IT IS THE WAY OF THINGS IN THE UNIVERSE

Leonidas

Let not others judge your way - the path you chose is the path you chose for a reason, there will be enough difficulty without them making it harder

Leonidas

The anticipation of happiness and the eagerness to feel its caress needs to be tempered with the knowledge of how to make it last forever.

Leonidas

Contents

Author's Note — Before we begin.....

The title of this book has been inspired by a Cat Stevens (Now called Yusuf Islam) song that is entitled "Oh Very Young". Every time I hear this song it reminds me of the Fragility of life and reminds me to live it while I have it. I encourage you all to listen to this song, read the lyrics and really take in Cat's (Yusuf's) meaning. He is truly a remarkable man...

Preface

This is not a story just of Geraldine who was diagnosed with cancer in July of 2007 and passed away from this disease on May 20th 2009, age 38 years old. It is the story of Leonidas who had to watch this person deteriorate physically yet grow so much spiritually during the period of the last two years of her life.

It is often said to me that she died young to which I always reply what does thirty eight mean? This is a human term not one that defines who or what she was. As humans we define time and limit ourselves to the time span we have on the earth's realm, in terms of our soul 38, even 138 is but the blink of an eye. In my way of thinking she achieved the ultimate goal in her time on earth; she achieved peace, happiness and become one with her spirit.

Remember that the term life is the lifespan you have in this incarnation. Your soul, which is eternal, includes the number of lifetimes it takes to learn all of its lessons. You can take as many or few lifespans you need to learn your lessons. Eventually you will learn them all and need not come back, allowing you to move to a higher level of existence.

When I am told she died young I usually ask the person, "how long is enough"? At what point are you happy to see someone leave this realm and enter into the next one? Is forever enough? To this I normally get a blank stare, but every now and then a person gets a spark of understanding in their eyes and nods really thinking about what I said – deeply thinking about it. To these people I say "you understand that the length of time is irrelevant it comes down to a simple question when you reach this point in time; are you going to go happy or sad?" It is this simple you will be at peace or not – there is no in between.

See this journey we embark on called life is exactly what it is called – life. It is for the living not those who are dead. Once they leave this realm they remain with you, but it is up to you to choose to be happy or sad this is YOUR CHOICE. To the ones who have moved on, it makes no difference if you choose to make yourself happy or sad, they are beyond this as they must leave this to you. Give them permission to help and they will, however you are in control.

Remember Death does not end life - it defines it.

Geraldine

I first saw this remarkable woman in 1988; our last year in high school. A mutual friend introduced us. I still remember one thing about that day with remarkable clarity, her eyes. She had enchanting eyes.

High school finished and we both went our separate ways and it wasn't until the end of 1989 that our paths would cross again. We ran into each other and that started a journey that changed the rest of my life.

Geraldine had gentleness about her; all in one I wanted to protect and inspire her to greater heights. She was someone that wanted my protection yet needed it not. I could see in her at that very moment the strength that she didn't realise she had, one that would guide her at the very end to be who she must. It didn't matter what facade she put on at the start (as we all do) I could see into her soul through those enchanting eyes, I could see all she could be and all that she wanted to be. After seeing that it did not matter if she wore a cloak of fear or anything else, I just needed to look into those eyes and I knew the true person. Once that happens neither of you can hide the truth of who you are.

How did I fall in love with her? That is simple my friends it is impossible to not when you have someone like Geraldine in your life. Looking back now it did take some time to actually fall in love; approximately 3.72 microseconds.

Geraldine was the type of person who was rare, one who could love unconditionally and accept you for who you were, even when you didn't know who you were yourself. There were times when she would just look at me and admire what she saw, there were times when she would trust me with her deepest fears and sadness, and at times she would show me her sense of humour that she showed to few others. These are the things that made me love her. All Geraldine needed was someone who could see the person she was, accept this person as a whole and love them completely. I think I had the easiest job in the world.

Geraldine didn't need much in her life as it was all about the simple things that she loved. I was privileged to have been allowed into her life. I know she said that I taught her to fly; a statement that still baffles me today as I really don't believe I did much. I always believed and believe still that she gave me far more than I ever gave her. I guess that is what would define a perfect relationship; both sides giving without effort and doing it unconditionally, not expecting a thing in return.

She was my everything and that made it all the harder to lose her, however when it is all said and done I have no regrets, not one. In fact if you were to ask me to do it all again I would do it in a heartbeat.

Pre finding out

We were always a happy and very close family; our beautiful children Caitlin, Daynon and Geordie and their adorable loving mother Geraldine. We did most things together as we did more than love each other; we actually liked each other – something I cannot say for all the couples I have seen in my journey.

I remember a number of times when people would say in passing that they would hate to be in business with their husband or wife as they would drive them nuts. I would always think to myself *I would love nothing more than to be in business with her, I would get to spend more time with her than I do now.*

One thing I need to comment on here is that Geraldine was always very spiritual; she had a manner about her that made her appear very angelic. She was always making the correct choices when she listened to her instinct. The problem for Geraldine was that she was afraid of the Spirit realm. She always had a block where she was not quite able to trust it implicitly. I had discussed this with her a number of times as I didn't share the same fear. I certainly didn't understand the Spirit realm, yet for some reason I felt very safe with it and had a trust in it. In the past whenever I trusted, the things I needed were given.

She would talk to me about how she felt and I would hear her say things like "I want to Paint" and she never would get around to it. I even remember buying all the canvases, paints and easels to start her off. They just sat there, seemingly something always got in the way. I tried pushing her at times but I would have to stop lest it end in an argument.

I reflect upon this now and think to myself *why be it that we always seem to avoid the passions in our lives and simply keep doing the routine that is getting us down in the first place?* It is amazing what can happen when you simply make the time to do those things that give you happiness. Humans are truly amazing at doing the things that are not good for us and terrible at choosing to make ourselves happy.

Being a close family was the most wonderful experience of my life. I always trusted and things appeared to be going along quite well. We had just moved in to our new house and our Children were all healthy. Geraldine had truly come through the depression caused by the issue that our middle child (Daynon) was born with a congenital heart defect and had to endure open-heart surgery at one week old. This shattered Geraldine and left her with Clinical depression – thankfully Daynon and his heart are perfect. This depression did not leave her easily. It got better with time, made easier by watching her child grow stronger; the final death throw for the depression was the birth of her beautiful son Geordie. She always had a special bond to him (I think it was a spiritual connection as in my view Geordie was given to her to help her heal). We always referred to him as the healing potion.

I recall in 2006 that Geraldine was very insistent on baptising her two sons, something that we had never gotten around to doing and probably wouldn't have bothered if our first child hadn't been baptised (It's more of a tradition in many Greek families than a religious thing to baptise children).

She seemed very driven to do this and I couldn't understand why. I just put it down to simply just wanting to get it done as she had had enough of people around her commenting on when she was going to do it. You see, Geraldine and I both suffered from a common ailment – not doing what makes you happy. We kept doing what others want or expect you to do to keep the peace.

I now believe the real reason she was driven to baptise her boys was not just the annoyance created by everyone else's opinion. It was that she had unintentionally tapped into her intuition and to her spirit guides who all knew that it was going to be the last chance she would get to do this. It's funny you know, eventually we all listen. Wouldn't it be nice if we chose to listen early enough to make a real difference to our lives? When are <u>you</u> planning on listening?

Finding Out

It all started with having difficulty swallowing. Around September 2006 Geraldine first noticed that sometimes food got stuck when she swallowed. She let it go at the beginning thinking nothing of it. In early 2007 the swallowing issue was becoming distressing for her. That's the first time I had the feeling; the one that occurred many times leading up to her death. It was a feeling in the solar plexus like someone had inserted some sort of device and was slowly tightening it. At this early stage it passed once she was able to swallow, once the problem had seemingly disappeared.

Eventually, we went to the doctor to get some help. She said it could be anything and not to jump to conclusions (then why do I keep on thinking to myself please don't be cancer?) and referred us to a clinic to get a gastroscopy.

We went to this clinic in March or April 2007. I remember taking her there and taking a book to read while I wait (little did I know it was to be the first of many such books to be read on my journey).

I was worried while I waited. The nurse came out and indicated to me that the procedure had all been done and she was OK. They were just having a little trouble waking her up from the anaesthetic (there's that twisting in the solar plexus again) but nothing to be concerned about. Geraldine came out and I took her home, it took her two days to recover from the Anaesthetic – Strange shouldn't take that long.

We awaited the results and finally got the news that the stomach and biopsies that were taken all came back normal; what a relief! Unfortunately it was the last relief we were to feel for a long time.

After this great news we just continued on with life. We still had to arrange to get some other tests done to find out why there still was the swallowing issue; we never got to those tests.....

I recall the time all so clearly, Geraldine was studying to sit exams for her Masters in IT (yet another thing she was doing that she didn't want to in her heart). She was doing this to get a better job and more money to allow our lives to be easier. This was partially my fault as I did encourage her to do this instead of pushing her to follow her dreams. You see I was trying to get ahead, little did I realise that to do this all Geraldine and I needed to do was let go of all the conditioning and trust that it will turn out alright. As long as we were happy and following our dreams, on our path and standing in our truth, everything would fall into place.

I came in to the room in which she was studying to find her lying on the ground feeling the area around her uterus and looking at me with a look from her soul that told me something was wrong, really wrong (there's that feeling again; the twisting in the solar Plexus). She asked me to feel it. I did, it felt like a golf ball sized lump. When I touched it a shiver of warning ran up my spine.

I re-assured her and we both decided to leave it for a little while. I have wondered at times if this waiting would have made a real difference in the end. Honestly I think not, the way the cancer progressed and moved I honestly don't believe that anything was going to stop it. More importantly this was her journey anything we did would have been lipstick on a pig. Dress it up any way you like; in the end it is still a pig – It is what it is; no matter how much you want it to be different.

Within the space of a week she grew in the abdomen like she was pregnant. Blind Freddy could see something was seriously wrong. I tried to convince myself she was pregnant, I even went as far as look into what sort of car we will need to have for a 6 person family. I would do anything to stop that nagging voice in my head warning me of the danger.

We went to see the doctor. She couldn't believe it was anything serious. In her view for it to grow so fast and be so big it must be a cyst (there's that twisting again). She referred us to an ultrasound clinic where we sat as the technician did his thing; he was taking an awfully long time. In the end he turned to us and confirmed that the mass was solid not fluid in nature (like a cyst would be). We went back to the doctor who referred us to a specialist to remove the "Cyst".

We didn't even make it to that visit; over the weekend Geraldine was so uncomfortable that I took her to the emergency ward and she was admitted in the hospital.

In Hospital

In hospital I kept on repeating to myself and Geraldine it's just a cyst, it's just a cyst, it's just a cyst. The doctor came and told us that he was going to do the surgery Monday night.

I remember wheeling her to the threshold of the automatic door to the operating theatre section of the hospital. That was the last time I saw my Geraldine Healthy again (Damn! That feeling again, twisting, twisting) oh well nothing to do but wait.

The nurse came to the room and said to me the doctor is on the phone for you. I walked to the phone expecting to hear that it was going to be alright – damn that twisting! The doctor told me in his superb way that he had removed Geraldine's ovaries and uterus as they had growths on them. That golf ball sized lump had grown to tumours of 15-20cm in size, in the space of two weeks.

He also indicated that her stomach "didn't feel right", don't you love doctors? Just scare the crap out of me without saying anything. I mustered up the courage to ask him what he didn't have the courage to tell me. "Is there any chance it is not cancer?" I asked. To this he said in his opinion it was cancer.

Geraldine came out of theatre and all I recall is her being drugged and asking me constantly did they get it all. Did they get it all? All I could do was cry and tell her yes however the twisting knot betrayed my lie.

The surgeon came to see us the next day and told us that the tumours were large and he removed both ovaries as well as her uterus, and again in his superb words to avoid having to say anything he said "we are in the hands of the pathologist to tell us what we are dealing with."

I kept on telling myself that it was nothing and the next day the surgeon came into the room, sat down on the bed and simply said "There is not an easy way to say this.....The cancer is stomach cancer and the tumours that we removed were secondary tumours." He couldn't give us any more information as this was not his area of expertise (He actually said quite jovially if it was ovarian cancer I could tell you all you want to know – YAY! thanks for that!) He referred us to another doctor and that was the last we saw of him for some time. In fact he was like the bearer of bad news – every time we went to him it always ended in something bad.

The other doctor came to see us the next day and started explaining to us what is going to happen from this point forward. Before I continue, I must say this doctor has to have been one of the nicest blokes I have met in my life and if he gives me permission I will name him at some stage. His manner and effort to save my Geraldine was superhuman. He kept us positive without telling us a lie. I really believe he could have told us from the very beginning that she had little chance yet he chose to tell us what we can do to get through rather than what we were up against. This was the kindest thing anyone could have done for us.

Upon reflection the only advice I can give is if you really don't want to know the answer don't ask the question. We always approached this disease with the attitude of think of what we want to achieve not the problems in the way. I think this was at the core of the length of time that Geraldine stayed on the earth. Remember a positive approach goes a long way towards healing.

Anyway I digress, the doctor proceeded to tell us how and when the chemotherapy was going to be administered and what side effect we could expect as well as what results we could expect.

I recall this moment in absolute clarity, you see this was my first and thankfully to now my only experience with anxiety. My whole body sized up I could only hear my heart beat, my breathing turned rapid and I was covered in sweat. My vision turned blurry, tunnelled and all I could see was the doctor. I just wanted to run screaming. The doctor looked at me and got very concerned, he asked me if I am OK and if I needed a glass of water. I quickly snapped out of it thinking to myself I have no right to be acting this way when Geraldine is the one who is going through it all. This thought helped me hold it together, that time and many times up until her death.

The doctor covered the side effects of the treatments. I won't bore you with the details you all have heard them before. In my simple terms you feel like crap and you go bald, essentially trying to kill the cancer without killing you in the process.

The tests started after this to confirm where the cancer was so it can be treated. After Gastroscopy, CAT scan, PET scan, Blood tests, stupid tests and any other damn test they could think of Geraldine felt like Pinky from Pinky and Brain the Lab rats (Looney Tunes – look it up). Fortunately she was given the best news possible for the situation - The cancer was only in the Stomach so the most likely result will be Chemotherapy followed by stomach surgery to remove the remaining Cancer.

Other Choices

For my part in this section of the saga I decided to look into alternative remedies. I know this is a contentious issue amongst many circles and I am not attempting to persuade people regarding these ideas. I will simply state my opinion and leave it to others to argue their own points of view. What I truly believe in my heart is that these "alternative" things all helped Geraldine last as long as she did, some even had the potential to save her in my view.

To those who will question some of these things I will discuss I say this to them: Why wouldn't you try something that may help? Does it matter that it is not proven? What if it does work for you? Just consider it, no one smart would tell you to do these things in place of the standard medical treatments, but why not augment them?

The things I researched fell into nutrition, treatment and spirit. Of these, with the benefit of hindsight, spirit gave us both the best results and assistance.

It is my belief that we spend too much time and effort healing the physical when we should be healing the soul. Even many spiritual endeavours are based in walking a spiritual path to heal the physical. Whilst this is a good idea, consideration should also be given to being spiritual in order to heal the soul, and then the physical can follow if it is meant to.

I was hell bent to find a cure for Geraldine. I just didn't want to leave this up to chance. I was sure there was something out there that could help her. I found a couple of things that I thought would help. I will list them below, however, I will go into limited detail of what they are or what they do; suffice to say in my opinion the nutritional changes made for Geraldine assisted in keeping her on this earth for long enough to get to where she needed to be. Those interested in the supplements should look in to them for themselves.

The things that were used consistently after Diagnosis were Apricot Kernels, Goji Juice, High intake of enzymes and Certain Vitamins as well as switching to a predominantly vegan raw vegetable diet. And most importantly all the food was organic.

Essentially the diet was rich in the things that cleansed your body and blood, anti-oxidants and enzymes all assist here. Minimizing the change in food from the way nature intended it was the basic intention. Organic produce to avoid introducing chemicals and toxins that are not meant to be there. As much raw food as possible; this is the closet way to what nature provides the food and none of the nutritional value, especially the enzymes that come naturally in the food, have been destroyed. Even when juicing we used a cold press juicer as the others momentarily heat the fruit and vegetables destroying the enzymes in them.

Essentially the more I investigated about nutrition and natural remedies the more I found that could help. I encourage you all to investigate these items for yourselves and make your own choices. You may be surprised at the results!

Spirit 1 – The beginning

Now for the spiritual side.

This started off my journey and led me to where I find myself today. I will start by explaining how it began.

I have always had an implicit trust of this realm, indeed this was something that always worked for me – things would just seem to work out for me because I asked them to. Little did I know that I was about to embark on a journey that would test this trust to its very limits and I can honestly say in the end the trust remains.

I was assisted on this path by a single person, one of my son's teachers, whom I remember telling of Geraldine's sickness and just in passing or as I now believe was guided to say to her "never mind I am sure the Spirits will provide." To this she replied with a look that pretty much looked in to my soul "do you believe in that?" after I said yes (and had a bit of a discussion) she gave me a card to someone that would change my life forever (yes I meant that - my life more than Geraldine's). This man was a medium and a healer (not to mention a top bloke).

I must at this point thank that person who put me in touch with the medium from the bottom of my heart. Through a very simple gesture you have changed my life and will always hold a special place in my heart – so THANK YOU!!(You know who you are).

I will return to this topic shortly but in the mean time I will bore you with some detail about going for treatments...

First treatment

The regime of treatment was to be some "magic" Chemotherapy drugs that I cared not to learn the name of. They were to be administered in cycles of 3 weeks for a total of 6 cycles. At the end of third cycle there were to be tests done to see how the treatment was progressing.

We turned up for the first treatment. The room was packed with bald people, over crowed in fact. I recall just trying to block it all out – too much noise can't cope!

I sat there and watched them sit down and explain how all the drugs worked, what you can and can't do... Don't go out in the sun all sorts of strange things. I remember watching the needle go in for the first time and putting it out there for angels to super charge the treatment.

The thing that kept on standing out in my mind was that we must have been the youngest there. I kept on saying to myself *why did it have to get her so young*? Ah well nothing to do for it - just fight!

Geraldine was amazing, as always, she simply took it in her stride (along with many things after this time). Without complaint she was poked, prodded and made to feel like crap but she just kept on taking it, stoically moving towards her goal. I have the utmost respect for someone who can stare death in the face and not move to deflect it but embrace what is coming and simply do their best to change the outcome.

After treatment she would go through the same cycle of events. She would feel tired after the first day as it was just a big day. Thanks to the litres of fluid that have been pumped into her during the treatment she would also look like someone had blown her up like a balloon. The fluid was meant to flush out her kidneys in order to protect them from the wonderful drugs being put in her (remember what I said about trying to kill the cancer without killing you in the process).

After this she would improve over the next few days. Just as she was about to feel close to normal again the regime of drugs would end dropping her into a semi-depressed state that was probably harder than the awful way the treatment made her feel. After the first week the next two were far better.

The most amazing thing to note here is that after the <u>very first</u> treatment the difficulty in swallowing went away; and no, it was not my imagination (or hers) she never had that issue again. She also developed hiccups quite regularly. I thought this was a good sign and asked the doctor. He said that there is no way it could have responded so quickly - I think Spirit had other ideas for her...

The diet changes at this point in time were more associated with the addition of the Goji Juice, Enzymes and the Apricot Kernels. These were our attempt to assist Geraldine; some of these items had helped other people I knew so we decided to take them. It is my belief that these items did indeed help.

Taking the advice of that dear special person, Geraldine called the Medium and Healer; he was incredibly warm and encouraging. He wanted to help and offered to do healings on Geraldine at no cost. The healings were always done by two people; they just wanted to help and genuinely knew they could assist. As much as the cost would not have mattered the gesture really was appreciated at the time as the cost of everything else was debilitating.

I recall the first time we went to get Geraldine's healing done. That twisting feeling that appeared part of my everyday life went away here. How odd. I came to find through the passage of time that it never appeared while I was at this place.

My first impression of this place was of the three people that were there regularly. The two men - one who always seemed to know what you were thinking, one who always had a joke and a lady.

The two men were amazing they just had an amazing way of knowing what Geraldine was feeling and where things were heading. They were very comforting. I found myself intrigued.

Anyway, a funny recollection of the healing was that one of the healers made the comment of what an awful taste she had in her mouth and the fact that she must have the runs (in fact it was the impersonation of not crapping himself that was funny). It was very funny on the surface but extraordinarily accurate. This was the first moment I really sat up and though there's got to be more to this.

To my end I just kept on researching and putting it out there that the result was going to be complete remission and my Geraldine will be fine. I just kept on putting it out there. After all, it had always worked in the past.

After 3 cycles of treatment (9 weeks) the moment of truth; the tests to see how the cancer was responding. Strangely I had a good feeling about this. We had to go through a CAT scan and a Gastroscopy.

I remember the Gastroscopy clearly. The waiting room air conditioner must have been set to about 2 degrees Celsius. Geraldine normally got cold; however, with the added bonus caused by the treatment she was very uncomfortable. I recall her saying to me in her cheeky way that she rarely showed to anyone that whatever brain cells had survived the Chemotherapy would have just been frozen – she always made me smile.

Funnily the doctor thought she was unwell and took her in earlier than her scheduled appointment – a blessing in disguise.

The three(ish) hours I waited were pretty tough, again reading those trusty books that I got to know so well.

Geraldine came out of the room and she took my arm and we walked outside. She told me that the doctor thinks it looks much better. She said "in the doctor's words: whatever you are doing continue to do it." I was speechless and all I could do was send a mental thank you to the Spirit world that came around to help her heal. We awaited the results of the Biopsies to confirm what the doctor had alluded to.

The results were not available until we went to see the Oncologist again. We waited in the waiting room for an eternity (45min actually). He came out and called us in and sat down in front of us looked at us blankly and said "it's gone" WHAT?? I said a tsunami of emotion threatening to explode out of my eyes. Well it does not show up in the CAT scan and the biopsies were all normal.

That knot in my solar plexus left me at that moment and didn't return for some time.....

We went through the rest of the treatments on a bit of a high. It was by no means a walk in the park but that was the physical side; mentally the last quarter of 2007 was pretty good.

The final part of the treatment was completed towards the end of November, we went through further Gastroscopies and CAT scans and also, I believe, a PET scan. These were all perfectly normal as expected and we were on cloud nine.

The doctor told us to go and enjoy the rest of our lives. We intended to.......

As part of the process we decided that we were going to organise a trip to Greece. Geraldine and I both really wanted to go back and see the place that gave us life and where our parents grew up. We decided to wait for a little while and go through the first round of follow up tests to ensure everything was OK prior to us going….We never got to go.

Spirit 2

As part of the changes made to our lives we continued to go for healings with what would later become some of my most trusted friends. After all, the doctor did indicate that her response to the chemotherapy was nothing short of amazing - didn't he?

We went there regularly and every time I went in there I would feel drawn to the place. A certain level of comfort and sense of belonging appeared to just fill me when I was there. I never really asked but I believe Geraldine felt the same way.

I recall little things like the way they would look straight into your soul and make just a little comment like have you been having pains in your Kidneys or something to that effect and you know that without fail they were spot on – fascinating.

I didn't pursue the spiritual side of it much at this stage. I didn't realise how much it was in fact helping us, I guess I just wanted to believe everything could go back to the way it was before Cancer - WRONG!!! Mistake number one! When you are given a lesson in life like the one that we had just received life is not meant to go back to the way it was before – that's what caused this crap in the first place! Easy to see that now but not so easy then, I guess I suffer from 20:20 Hindsight like everyone else.

I kept having a nagging voice in my head telling me to look into what these guys are about and see if they can do anything for me. I didn't; I guess I was scared?

No not really scared I just always seemed to find an excuse to put it off. The situation I was in made the decision to pursue this difficult, however, if I was to be really honest I also just wanted to avoid really looking into my soul as I might have found things that I really didn't like. You see hiding from these truths often provide false comfort to people allowing them to survive in this world. I implore you to all take the time to look into your soul and see what is there. If you don't like what surfaces you have an opportunity to fix it rather than walking through life wondering why you are not satisfied.

This is the basic premise; the reason you are on this earth - to learn, grow and heal your soul. <u>You</u> have chosen to incarnate with particular lessons to learn this time around. If you don't fulfil them or learn them it has only then been a truly wasted life.

Spirit was something Geraldine was happy to have help and assist her; however, the trust was not there for her to embrace it fully. Who knows what the outcome would have been if she did? Was this one of her lessons and challenges? Only she will truly know the answer to this now.

Spirituality at this stage was really an introduction, a taste that left the nagging thought in my head that I wanted to further explore it. I just did not seem to find the time until much later on – excuses, excuses – there was always something else to do or place to be just when I wanted to follow these things up.

Happy times!

The happiest moment for Geraldine since she was diagnosed with Cancer to her death was the period straight after her first Chemotherapy treatment. It was the period of December 2007 through to around May 2008. This was the time that we truly thought she had won.

We had gone for a number of tests and everything was clear – she was my superwoman! Even the doctor had said that the result she had achieved and the response she had to chemotherapy was amazing.

We had a fabulous Christmas that year; full of Joy and Happiness and full of the possibilities of the future. New Year was like a breath of fresh air out with the horrible 2007 on to a happy and prosperous 2008. We even went to Mallacoota that year and I recall Geraldine proudly walking around with her skinhead style hair cut looking something like one of the characters out of Romper Stomper. I recall thinking how beautiful she looked regardless of the short hair. She always looked beautiful, she just had a way of carrying herself and looking at you, she was a striking woman.

This time was an interesting test for us as we did change however it was not quite enough.

Geraldine still felt all the emotional baggage that got her to this point. Issues around her childhood still plagued her, yet she continued to deny the call from her inner self to deal with them. As for me I was still finding out reasons to avoid finding out more about what those healers do (even though that voice keeps on telling me to!)

I must say that to most of the people looking in the issues Geraldine faced on the surface would be considered trivial. Even I at times would wonder why they hurt her so.

The point is, it matters not what you or I think about the issues that impacted Geraldine, only that to her they were major and they did bother her. For my part, I could see how they bothered her, so it was not necessary to understand them or judge her as to why. It was however extraordinarily important to support her in whatever it took to get her over them.

Please, please, please remember not to consider other people's issues from your perspective. It is the person's very perspective that makes them an issue in the first place after all. If they had your perspective they possibly wouldn't have the issue to begin with, would they?

Spirit 3

It was around March or April in 2008 when Geraldine was talking to one of our dearest friends in fact we were over at their house having dinner. One of them mentioned a person they have heard a lot about. This man was a Kinesiologist and apparently very good at what he did.

I would like to think of myself as an intelligent person and I classify myself a sceptical yet open person. I am open enough to try anything but I need to see some sort of evidence for myself to believe it; boy did I get it here!

We called up and went to see the Kinesiologist – apparently very hard to get an appointment with but there just happened to be an available slot perfect for Geraldine. Funny how things appear at the right time when needed isn't it?

We went in there and sat down. He spoke to us for a while about what he does and how it all works, it sounded unbelievable but being open I thought I am just going to observe and see what happens.

The Kinesiologist got Geraldine to lie down and started doing all these hand gestures and moving Geraldine's hands and arms. I was watching it with interest, fascinated, (my quirky sense of humour flashed up the image of the commercial teasing alternative remedies – it was of a Russian guy waving two fish over a lady and slapping them together – HBA I think) I am not for a moment saying this was rubbish, actually quite the opposite. In fact, I have been seeing this person on and off since that time and he is probably on the list of my five people who saved me on the journey I have travelled so far.

As I was saying; he was doing his hand manoeuvres and doing all sorts of movements. I was sitting behind him wondering what on earth he was doing when he suddenly said to Geraldine. "What happened to you when you were 28?"

I started to count back to work out what year it was (1999). As I was doing that she said without hesitation and beginning to cry "my son was born with a congenital heart defect" Now you need to remember that this man did not know either of us from a bar of soap.

After I got up from falling out of my chair, closed my mouth and re- inserted my eyeballs that had fallen out, my complete focus was on this guy as he worked to remove the emotion that was locked away in Geraldine.

This was a turning point for me I knew that I was going to see this man to help me on my journey and I also knew at that moment that I needed to explore that side of me. I still made many excuses before I actually did it.

I will say it again this man was and still is one of the stabilising forces in my life.

Back Again

I remember it all too clearly, the day the twisting in my solar plexus returned. I don't recall the date very well; I do clearly remember the situation.

Geraldine had gone to the toilet she came out and said to me that she could really feel her bladder when it was empting especially right at end. Wham! Cold all over on my little twisted friend in the solar plexus has returned with vengeance.

I tried to convince her that we all get that feeling every now and then. I think I managed to convince her and myself – For approximately 3 microseconds. The look in her face betrayed the truth and my twisted friend betrays my lie.

We meandered along in denial for around a month, probably because we didn't want to face the truth. We even mentioned it to the Oncologist who did not think it was anything to worry about. All our scans and tests were clear and she was going from strength to strength. "After all" he said, "You will get complaints that are not cancer related." Ironically from this point on everything she felt was cancer related.

Anyway, we went for a urine test to see if she had an infection; Nothing. The doctor suggested we go back to the original doctor who did the surgery on Geraldine to check it out (remember what I said about this guy and every time we saw him it was bad news? – correct again). Damn that twisting Knot.

We went to see this doctor on a Friday – I recall it well as we had to drive quite far to a clinic he attended on Fridays. I recall waiting and wondering what was going to happen. I was screaming in my head that everything was going to be alright, I refused to accept anything else. With the twisting in my solar plexus we went in and the doctor saw us.

He was reviewing the file and seemed genuinely surprised to see us. At the time I thought it was because she was in remission but now I believe he was surprised for other reasons (the fact that she was still alive). Anyway he listened to the complaints of feeling odd in the bladder when urinating.

The Doctor got Geraldine up on the examination table and did an internal exam. He indicated that a certain area did not feel completely right (famous words from this guy). He wasn't too concerned; he thought there was a little thickening in the lining of the uterus and that it may just be the way she is built. He also did a Pap smear and noted that there was no blood – a good sign. He told us to go away and come back in 6 weeks to see if there are any changes. We left convincing ourselves to feel relieved. My twisted friend in the solar plexus was having a field day making it hard to feel any peace.

July 19th 2008 was the day when my world and that twisting feeling reached the point where it felt like I was actually going to have a mental breakdown. The day was actually the day of both my son's birthday parties and I recall this day as if it were yesterday.

Geraldine was a little withdrawn that day, she was quiet at the best of times but something about the way she carried herself looked strange. I did ask her if she was OK. She of course, as always, said she was OK (gosh she never complained – even though if anyone deserved to it was her). I thought she had withdrawn as at other times just because she wanted to process stuff on her own, I always tried to give her space to do this. But why did this time feel a little different.

I took my boys to the party and Geraldine was to follow with my brother a little later (being fashionably late as she always was). She ended up getting to the party about half way through it. By this stage I was wound up like a spring, really, really worried. She turned up and I could see she was not comfortable. She was holding her abdomen and was clearly in pain but my hero did not flinch she stayed to watch her son's party.

We got home after the party along with some friends. I was beside myself with fear. It is probably the closet I have ever come to a complete and utter mental break down. I couldn't even process what people were saying to me. All I could do was to try and help Geraldine. You see she hadn't gone to the toilet for a couple of days, yep good old constipation. We went to the hospital as it was getting bad; as soon as we got there she went to the toilet for about half an Hour and felt decidedly lighter.

After this relief we left feeling a little silly (and lighter). Remember what I said earlier about ironically everything she felt after that point in time was cancer related – Correct again! We did not know it at the time but this was too. At least we had a short period of relief. After that she never pooed normally again.

We spent the next six weeks analysing everything that was occurring, hyper-sensitive to what was going on. I guess deep down we both knew that there was something wrong; we were just trying to hide from it.

The day for the second visit came. The doctor did the same check and was not satisfied with what he felt. He wanted to wait longer but we asked him "are you concerned about it?" He replied "in my opinion it does not feel right" OK why didn't you just say that to begin with Einstein?

He looked at our faces and said "you look ambivalent so I will do a cystoscopy to find out what is going on or if there is anything to worry about" (He loved big words this bloke I think he hid behind them). I hope ambivalent means scared to death otherwise my expression was not accurately read.

I was concerned when we went to the hospital for the cystoscopy. Both Geraldine and I had a horrible feeling. Realistically, I think we both knew that we were in for trouble on some level. I sat in the room holding her hand, wishing, asking, and pleading for it to be nothing. The nurse came in a wheeled her away. That was the last time I saw Geraldine without cancer again.

I sat in the hospital room by myself on a single chair in the spot where the bed was just a short while earlier, without anything else really in the room. I tried to read my book but I just couldn't focus, I could hear my heart beat, I could feel the sweat running down my armpits. My old friend Mr Twisty in the solar plexus was dancing a jig. I just waited for the surgeon. I felt as lonely as the image you are imagining.

The surgeon came and again he managed to say lots without saying anything – I love this guy – anyway he had a hard job to do so I don't envy his position. He told me that they found some abnormalities in the bladder. *Abnormalities?* I thought to myself, why can't this guy just speak in English!? So I found myself asking (again) is there any chance it is not cancer. I remember him saying the growths were hard, they felt a bit like the round knobby bit of the bone in your wrist or ankle – this was consistent with cancer. He had taken biopsies (I guess we were in the hands of the pathologist again).

Geraldine came back and she just looked at me; she didn't have to ask the question to which she already knew the answer. I just said to her we will beat this OK? No giving up? I will stand next to you, carry you and nurse you...But you will get through this OK?

Her Oncologist came to see me and his reaction was something that really touched me and made me realise how tough it must be for someone to do what he does. He just looked at me and said "When I was told I just wanted to leave work and go home and drink a bottle of scotch" I felt exactly the same way. He also said "I really thought we had beaten it you know? She was my star patient." In my opinion she was and always will be a star.

Spirit 4

I always trusted the Spirit world. Every choice I made to assist and guide Geraldine I did mostly on instinct and on what I felt was the right course of action. I did this for the choice of supplements as well as the choice of alternative therapies that she should try.

I encouraged her to meditate to become at peace with herself and truly discover her spirit within. Most of all I wanted her to deal with the issues of the past but somehow I knew the path to this was through her understanding and acceptance of her spiritual side.

I suggested ways for her to meditate, to start to believe that the universe was looking after her and she just had to accept who she was to assist her in healing.

Her fear was what held her back. You see, if you trust and give permission to the Spirit world it will help, however, you are the key to allowing it in. It is by your choice to give them permission that they can help. I didn't know this then and couldn't articulate it as well as I just did.

It is around this time she started to seriously explore some of the spiritual healing techniques. Most of these that attracted her were more about regressing to the past to see what issues pop up that need to be dealt with. Some amazingly powerful tools were learnt here.

Oh and she finally picked up that paint brush and started to paint. In fact, the cover of this book is the painting she finally did.

I will speak more of what Geraldine did later. At this point I need to make a mention of a friend of my family who I could say is probably one of the dearest people on the face of this earth. From the moment she found out about Geraldine's condition to now she was and is a rock for both of us and for me after Geraldine's death.

She shared some of this spiritual journey with Geraldine and got to really understand how she thought. I consider her both privileged to have met the true Geraldine (few, very few people on this earth were given that privilege by Geraldine) and extraordinarily special to be able to support us both as she did. To her I say I love you I thank you and I will be your friend forever.

Treatment

We went to our next appointment with our oncologist and he explained to us that given the cancer had come back he could not offer us a cure at this point in time. All he could offer was control of the disease.

Geraldine would be going through the same chemotherapy treatment as the first time, a prospect that she was very frightened of as she now knew what she was about to go through. She asked the doctor if it would make a difference if she waited around four weeks before she started treatment. He was hesitant but allowed her to do this.

During this time Geraldine went to many nutritionists for advice to see if there was something she could do to get the edge over this horrible disease. They all were useful but she always struggled with the amount of supplements she needed to take. At one stage they had her eating up to 30 pills a day.

She was attracted to the Gawler foundation as it used spiritual as well as a nutritional supplement regime. A friend of ours also handed her Brandon Bays "The Journey". I recall Geraldine reading it from cover to cover intently fascinated by it. She was determined to explore this side now. I was so proud of her and gave her as much encouragement as I could.

One thing I have glossed over is the issue of going to the loo. Let me just say in passing that it landed her in hospital twice, once for the period of a week. Both times it was said it was just constipation – Constipation my arse!

We went to another doctor to get a second opinion, he gave us some ideas of what we could try and we ran them all past our oncologist, unfortunately he had thought them all through and none of them were viable.

The reason for her having difficulty going to the toilet as well as the reason for needing Chemotherapy as a treatment again was simple; the cancer was not just in the bladder it was in the lymphatic system as well. This was causing a build-up of fluid in her abdomen, causing her bowels not to work properly. It also meant that radiotherapy on the bladder would not get it all.

Her best chance was to control it and stay on some medication to keep it under control. We got the fluid drained - 2 Litres or thereabouts (lovely). I recall the day after this draining that she came downstairs and proudly announced that she was able to go to the toilet normally. Strange how a simple thing that nobody thinks twice about can make someone so happy.

She had booked in to the Gawler foundation to do the residential program. Sadly she never got to this as the fluid built up too quickly and she had to start treatment as soon as possible. She always intended to go back and do the course. This was not to be.

She started her treatment around September, again she was to have a test after the third cycle and see how she was progressing.

We started the treatment, after the very first one I recall her being up at the toilet urinating all night. It appeared to be far more than what would have occurred just because of the amount of fluid they put in her. It really did appear like her bladder was reacting to something. We mentioned this to the doctor and he replied that he did not believe that she would have had such an immediate reaction.

Spirit 5

The odd thing here was that I was sure the treatment was working from the very first moment. There just seemed to be an air of healing around Geraldine.

I remember going to the healers and they were both very focused on getting her through this. Something about them had changed. Maybe they could sense this was truly a hard one to win and they were stepping up what they were doing? Maybe I was just becoming more in tune with what they were doing?

I know one thing I could see; Geraldine was going into the healing flat and tired and came out with the spark of life firmly in her eyes. For that alone I must say thank you to all of those wonderful people who helped her, it was comforting to see her come out better every time.

For my part at this stage I was really starting to think I should go and do some work with these people and learn what they do. I started to talk to some of the people at the school and found it more and more fascinating.

Still, the timing wasn't right, the good old excuses kept on coming up. I recall telling Geraldine on the way home from her healing that I really want to explore what they do. She looked at me and fixed me with her look and simply said you should. Still I found excuses.

Remission?

The more time went on the more I was convinced that it was actually working. Her belly seemed to stop growing with fluid and it actually started to get better. The doctor was very conservative in his view but I was pretty sure that we were going to be alright.

After the third cycle of treatment we were booked in for another cystoscopy – more time to read books. I was waiting for Geraldine for around three or four hours when the nurse came and told me that she was about to go and get her from recovery.

I thought my heart was going to explode! I saw her wheeled in and was trying desperately to gauge how it went from the expression on her face. I kept on trying to get a glimpse of her but the nurse kept getting in the way, finally she saw me and her face lit up; I knew at that moment it had all gone well.

She told me that the Doctor said it was amazing (I was getting used to this from her by now) it was completely gone, he had taken biopsies just to be certain but it looked normal.

We went back to the oncologist about a week later and he said to us "It's gone – biopsies normal." What great news! I remember the first thing Geraldine did was point to the device that was implanted and said "I want this porta-catheter out."

A Porta-Catheter was a device implanted under your skin so they could plug a special needle in for the Chemotherapy to be delivered.

Unfortunately this sat near the breast, stuck out and was quite visible. Geraldine really was limited in what she could wear let alone every time she looked into the mirror all she would see was this reminder – she hated it. She had left it in the first time so she could confirm she was in remission prior to taking it out. This time it was coming out as she didn't want to know about it.

It was nice to have that horrible thing out even though it was short lived.

We now found ourselves leading up into the Christmas period. We all went away for both Christmas and New Year. It wasn't as exciting as the previous year; all we really felt was some relief and exhaustion. I have never wished as hard as I did that New Year's Eve in my entire life. I pleaded to whoever wanted to listen for health. I guess I was scared because I had a sense that something was up; maybe there was intuition working here?

Intuition and the fact that her belly never looked right again. It just seemed bloated at times, and she still had difficulty going to the toilet (Mr Twisty is dancing in my solar plexus again).

We got through the Christmas and New Year period and went back to the doctor in early January. He was sure that there was not fluid in her belly; then why was it distressing us both so much?

We ended up getting an ultra sound done which confirmed there was a lot of liquid in the belly. This was drained and we had the news we were dreading confirmed. There were cancer cells in the fluid again. That twisting feeling was now pretty much a constant companion now.

After Geraldine got the fluid drained she was on a high – everything worked normal again! She was up and about and fighting fit. That was until that fluid returned.

We went to the doctor and he ordered a CAT scan, we went to do this not really knowing what to expect. Nothing really showed up on this scan apart from a narrowing of the tube between the Kidney and the bladder. She would lose the use of the kidney if the tube was not supported by surgically inserting a catheter to drain the urine. Another surgery, more books read!

She came through this with flying colours! The doctor confirmed that the bladder was still clear! That was the ironic thing about this cancer; wherever it was beaten it never returned, unfortunately it also spread like a wild fire.

Spirit 6

At this point in time (January 2009) I had a conversation with Geraldine. It was probably the hardest thing I have ever had to do.

I sat down with her and I remember my words clearly. I said to her "Babe, I have done everything I can for you up until now; I have tried to guide you and push you to where you need to be. This now is your Journey, you need to do this for yourself, and you need to find your way and your own path. I may have brought you to the cliff's edge but you need to take the leap of faith. I am going to step back and you are going to take control of your life and take it in any direction you want."

With this, I now know, I had to step aside to allow her to prepare for death. To her credit she did. I had to let her do it; I had to let my beloved go. If that was what she needed to do, who was I to stand in her way? I loved her enough to give her this.

She still had a number of months to live. I must say these were probably the most profound months in her life.

As far as treatments go there is nothing much more to be said about this matter - they tried stuff and it didn't work; that's all. I will only mention hospital again towards the end.

I recall a conversation I had with her about what would happen if she did not make it (I hated these conversations) I remember her looking at me and saying: "I want you to promise me that you will move on if I don't make it." I said to her that I would, I promised, I said "I am not sure how I will do it, yet I will and I will also make sure that the Kids do as well." The response she gave me to this made me stop in my tracks, I still recall clearly; she held up her hand and simply said with an amazing air of authority "I am at peace with the kids – I have no doubt they will be OK" (strange thing for someone to say who was fighting to live).

During this time I recall she had some conversations with her Mother about certain issues she had, after this time she seemed to have a bit of weight lifted off her shoulders. With me not being as involved in everything, her sisters stepped in around her and helped take her to appointments and also asked the doctors questions to understand what was going on and what they could do to help.

I don't know if they realised but this period was the time that Geraldine made peace with respect to her family. After this moment she had released any issues she had and made her peace with the person who mattered the most; herself.

During this time she was instinctively preparing herself for death. She did a number of things that I believe changed the course of her finding peace.

Geraldine attended a journey workshop in March of 2009. This allowed her to find some of the issues that were buried deep inside. I am told those who search for these issues can often be very surprised at the source of the emotional problem. Geraldine chose not to share with me in great detail what she dealt with that day. It was clear that it took a burden off her shoulders and that was enough for me.

Interestingly after she attended the workshop I found her at times giving me advice. When I would take too much emotional stuff on she would say "stop taking it on, leave it with them." It was interesting that even in her current state she was able to give advice on this. She certainly seemed to slow down and appreciate things more. I would often catch her just observing her children really just trying to take them in.

Meditation was something she did about an hour every day. It was an integral part of Geraldine finding some peace. Out of all the processes she attempted, I believe meditation gave her the greatest understanding and peace. It is the foundation upon which all healing and peace is built. I don't believe she would have achieved any of what she did without using the meditation as the base.

She continued to go to the Healers, what can I say? We really didn't know what they were doing. I was aware however, that she always left feeling lighter than when she came. That was enough for me to know that it was helping.

I recall one time when the female healer did the healing. I was in the same room, I decided to close my eyes and see if I could lend some energy to help Geraldine heal. At the time I really didn't have a clue what I was doing or if it would help. I know now that lending or giving energy in that way assists the healer by allowing a larger energy pool for them to draw on to deliver the healing. Half way through the healing she turned to me and said "you should do the Reiki course; you could then heal Geraldine whenever you want".

With the knowledge I have now, I am not surprised with what she said. I was however, really startled by it at the time. It was at that moment that I said to myself I am going to work with these guys, I don't know when or how, yet I am going to do it. I just put it out there, at that moment I made a commitment to the Spirit world. For those who know me also know that the commitment is being fulfilled (thankfully).

The other thing that I had no way of knowing at the time was that this was the last healing that Geraldine was to receive from these people.

She also continued to see her Kinesiologist who continued to have an amazing way of digging out those hidden emotions that were eating away at her. He continued to help her to release these emotions. She had many moments of tears but each and every one was one less burden she was going to have to face, one less thing to hold on to.

It was around the end of March or Mid-April when I came home from work one day and Geraldine simply looked at me and said "I need you back (in my life) now". I said to her it would be my pleasure (in truth it was probably the end of the hardest thing I had ever had to do. I had to sit back and not try to help while someone I cared for navigated their way through their stuff). I simply re-engaged.

One thing I would like to note here is that I feel Geraldine truly figured it out. Our journey is to heal our soul which she did. This allows us to be at peace when we cross over. Healing of the physical is a by-product of the soul healing and indeed only if it is meant to be that way. You are ultimately here to heal your soul. Once done you can cross or stay and have further journeys knowing that this lesson has been achieved and finished.

The one thing that she kept during this last period was a diary - I believe a couple of people suggested that she should keep one.

I found the diary after her death and I will not disclose what was in it apart from a couple of things including the extract below which showed me that she made her peace. This is the only important point to the diary that she used it as a tool to make peace with herself. Its contents were and still remain irrelevant to us. After all making peace with yourself is the only thing you owe to yourself.

Geraldine's own words:

I am grateful for all the gifts I have

- My children
- Leon (Leonidas)
- My extended family (sometimes)
- This moment in time
- All the wonderful people I have met on my healing journey
- Moments when I sit and watch my children and their beautiful mannerisms
- My special Friends
- The gift of healing

I AM NOW HEALING IN MIND, BODY, SPIRIT AND EMOTION

The following is a translation of a poem written in the diary by Geraldine during this time. It was written in Greek and I have translated it, I trust it has the same impact in English as it does in Greek.

The Little Girl

From young she learnt to be alone
She never said much
Yet she observed all
And kept it all in her heart.

Sensitive from the beginning
She knew the thoughts of others without them saying a word
And she couldn't understand
Why there wasn't more love to be found.

Her life seemed scary to her
Like a little bird
Too afraid to fly
From the cage.

All the wonderful things around her
She held on to none of them
Fear being her constant companion
With difficulty she walked through life.

As time went by
And she found her man
Who showed her the path
To allow her wings to fly

I need to comment about this poem, I need to say thank you to Geraldine for taking the time to pen such beautiful words. Truly I did not know that I had such a profound impact on her life, indeed I always thought that she had a greater impact on me then I did on her. This poem helped validate what I believed and allowed me to move on.

There was a moment in time when I think marked the beginning of the end for Geraldine. I was sitting watching TV with her one day; I remember my thoughts went to what she had been through, the way she carried herself, the way she found peace. All of a sudden I turned to her looked her in her eyes and said" Babe I am so proud of you, you are my hero – I just want you to know that." She simply looked at me smiled and simply said "thank you." It was the last time I saw Geraldine smile (a least in this realm). A month later she entered the Spirit world.

The month leading to her end on this earth can be described in many words; the only one that I wish to use is sad, that is all.

For a little while she was getting a pain in her hip and it would travel down her leg. We mentioned it to the Oncologist who said it was likely a tumour pushing up against a nerve (Yay). This pain was quite debilitating for her and she never really was able to get around adequately after it appeared.

I would come home and find her lying in bed or sitting in the same chair for most of the day. It was sad to see someone so full of life limited in this way. I would try and cheer her up by being silly (she always laughed at that). No response, she spent the whole time pre occupied, she lost her opinion on things, and she just went along with whatever anyone said.

It strikes me now that she knew where she was heading and was busily preparing herself. She was not concerned about the usual things like when she ate and went to doctors for she was on a far more important path.

Around this time she was admitted to hospital for the pain. They pumped her full of morphine and this was barley taking the edge off the pain. She was in Hospital for a total of a week where they ascertained that it had travelled to the bones near the base of the spine and also in the hip area.

Around Easter Geraldine did her course of Radiotherapy which knocked her about far more than it should have.

She was out of hospital for Greek Orthodox Easter which was a week after the conventional Easter but she was not herself. She really just sat in a chair and could hardly move around.

We were staying at her mother's house so she could assist Geraldine. Another thing I noticed was after the stint in hospital Geraldine's voice was Slurred and she didn't even sound like herself.

She was down to around 39 Kilos, slurring her words, vague not really engaging in life. In fact quite the opposite.... She was preparing to move on.

The one thing I need to say is that staying in the hospital caused her to lose a lot of condition. She easily lost about 8kg in the space of a week. She was hardly awake throughout the whole stay. With hindsight it would have been better to have kept her at home.

The palliative care nurse pulled me aside for a chat. She was the first person to approach the subject that she may not make it through. I was pretty stubborn about it but in the end I could do nothing but acknowledge that she may be correct. It broke my heart.

Through this period of time Geraldine stopped going to her healers and all the other people that were helping her. She always used the excuse that she was not able to move or was in too much pain. It was a legitimate reason but I think there was more to it; she was simply preparing herself for death.

I need to mention all the healers at this point for preparing her space to allow her to move on easily when the time came. I now know there was quite a bit of effort put in to making her transition simple, peaceful and quick, for that I will be forever grateful.

Everyone was trying everything to keep her going. In the end all I could do was sit with her, hold her and tell her I was there. I had accepted the final outcome was not going to be what we had wanted. I realised I couldn't change it so I had to just accept and surrender to the will of the Universe.

I decided that the only constructive thing I could do was to try and prepare my children for what I thought was coming. I recall sitting down with my daughter and looking at her and saying "Mum's in trouble Babe" I sincerely hope I never see that look on her face ever again. She started to cry and I said to her "she is going to fight and I am going to do everything I can to help her, I just don't know if she is going to make it." She had a good cry but I am so glad I had the conversation with her as it gave her a chance to prepare. I had a similar conversation with the boys but being a bit younger I kept it much simpler (and they are male after all) and told them that she is going to struggle to make it and reassured them that I intended to live for a very long time (to annoy them). They amazingly took it in their stride.

The Friday before her death Geraldine had a visit from the Palliative care nurse. She noted that she was bed-ridden and seemed a bit dehydrated. She wanted to take Geraldine into the Palliative care hospital where they could help get her pain under control and get her re-hydrated. I re-call this as I received some phone calls asking me to allow her to go to the hospital.

Geraldine flatly refused to go, she told the Nurse there was no way and told me the same thing earlier on in the week. I had an interesting conversation with the nurse where I was telling her bring whatever they needed to the house and hydrate her there. She continued to say she should really come into hospital until in the end I said "look if she is going to die she has chosen to do it at home OK? There is no way in hell I will allow you to go against her wishes and take her to the hospital!"

Needless to say the issue was dropped after this and they tried their best to help her from home.

I was standing in my front yard about two days before Geraldine died, I was thinking about her predicament. All of a sudden I looked up at the stars thinking about what was coming to pass and I recall saying to whoever cared to listen "If there is no chance for her please take her quickly, she has suffered enough."

They were listening.

19th May 2009

I gave Geraldine some strong pain killers in the evening as recommended by the doctor. These knocked Geraldine completely out. Her GP came over for a routine visit to see how she was going, she was a little concerned with her state but put it down to the Pain Killers.

I helped Geraldine to bed and lied down beside her and watched her breathe. This is the image I fell asleep to.

20th May 2009

I woke up with a start at 5:15 am to find Geraldine breathing very shallow and rapidly, her extremities were also very cold. I huddled up against her to try to warm her up. After sometime without it working I decided to go downstairs and get a hot water bottle for her. I stopped dead in my tracks with a shiver running down my spine. My clock in the Kitchen had stopped at 5:15 am. I made sure the clock started again, corrected the time and went upstairs with the hot water bottle.

There were a number of medical people who came in and out that day; they bear little importance in this discussion so they have been left out on purpose....

I spent the next couple of hours lying with my high school sweetheart and kissing her brow telling her that I love her, that was all I could think of and I am sure that was all she wanted. She would reply between the puffs of air......love.....you...too. I knew what was coming and I had to simply let the universe take her and break my heart.

At around 11:30 am on the 20th of May my Geraldine uttered the words......Hold.......my.......hand..... I took her hand; she fixed me with a look, one of almost disbelief. I looked at her and said "Babe I love you, we all love you and we will never forget you, but it is your time. However, do something for me, go happy please don't go sad". I said to her I love you, and she said love......you and her eyes rolled in her head.

Geraldine left this world at that moment and was finally free of that disease. I remember saying to her dead body later on, well done babe you finally beat it because where you have gone that monster can't follow.

I left to get some oxygen as recommended earlier by the Palliative medical people knowing that she had already passed but not willing to accept it. My mother rang me up in a panic and said that Geraldine was not well I told her to call an ambulance and I headed back. By the time I got there she had been pronounced dead by the paramedics. She passed about half an hour earlier is what he said to me. What a surprise I was gone for about that long.

This period of time after her death became a blur, I only recall telling her how proud of her I was and noting how different her body looked without her in it. The only other thing I recall was our family doctor hugging me and explaining to me how amazing it was that she fought it for so long. If I recall correctly she said people with that sort of cancer at the stage it was usually only got between 5 weeks and 5 months. She got it in remission for 6 months and fought it for a total of two years – a truly remarkable effort by a truly remarkable Human.

The first thing that needed to be done was tell the children. How the hell do I do this? How the hell do I tell them they have just lost their mum? At this point I was so glad I had given them some preparation earlier on and had said to them that she was in trouble.

I went to my boys first at their primary school. I remember sitting in the principal's office for the first time in my life when I wasn't in trouble (how I wished I was there because I had misbehaved). I saw my boys coming and I prepared myself.

I looked at my boys and I said to them I don't really know how to tell you this but you know how mum was struggling with cancer? Well she lost her fight today boys, your mum has died. I can tell you that she isn't suffering anymore which is a good thing, but I am so sorry for you". They didn't say much I just assumed it was the shock, now I believe on some level they were expecting it. Now to tell the next one....

I knew this was going to be the hardest one, my daughter. I sat in another office for the second time in my life without being in trouble but again feeling a much larger sense of dread.

My daughter showed up already crying, I just held her and cried with her and said "I am so sorry this has happened - just remember she loves you and she tried her best." She was quite upset (understandably) and then all of a sudden she stopped and looked at me and asked "are you going to find someone else?" I replied indicating that it is probably not the right time to be talking about it but since she brought it up I asked her what she thought about me finding someone else. She replied with "I think you deserve to." Caitlin, I need to express to you how much those words meant, I thank you for helping me move on. I appreciate your support; you are a very special person and my friend.

The rest of the day was a procession of grief from others expressing all sorts of things. For my part the next couple of days were surreal I have been asked often what I felt the days just after she died? I have thought about it a lot and the main thing I felt was relief, for me, for her and relief for everyone. I felt very tired as if a major weight had been lifted from my shoulders and I just needed to sleep (kind of like forest Gump when he said I'm pretty tired – I think I'll go home now).

We had many people come to visit and express their sympathies, all of this was welcome. The reactions that really meant something to me were from those who genuinely knew Geraldine and who she was, these people included parents at the school and some of our relatives. Their reaction to the death of this beautiful person was something that will always hold a special place in my heart. They were not merely sad, they truly felt as though a stabilising force had left their lives; someone who they could turn to in their moment of despair and know the wisdom that sprung forward form this person would help them through whatever situation they were travelling at that time.

I sat down with the kids to give them my perspective on what happened. I gave them an analogy; "You know how when you step out of the car it stops working? Well Mummy stepped out of the body she was using and it doesn't work anymore. She is still around us and she did the only thing she could do to ensure that she could continue to look over you, she had to go to the Spirit world." They seemed to understand this and I also added that they were destined to meet her again and probably have a future life with her when the time was right. I also said to them that this was my belief system and they were free to believe anything they wished.

I recall having to make calls to so many people and tell them that she had passed; this I did with relative ease. After a certain point you become numb and the words just come out as if someone else is saying them. You can hear people crying but you almost don't know why. It is just a blur...

As mentioned earlier there was relief and exhaustion initially; as time went on it was replaced by my mood swings from happy to uncontrollable grief. I allowed it all to happen as I realised that to hide from it and avoid it was the easy but incorrect way. I allowed the emotions to wash over me as they came up without moving to avoid them or shift them. I had a belief that eventually they would pass and I would be able to celebrate her life rather than grieve her death. I was correct.

I recall finding the diary Geraldine was keeping, it was about two days after she had passed and I saw it in a cupboard. It was a book I got for her to write in and I had no idea that she had been writing in it. I started to read it and came across many interesting comments about things from her past, as well as the day to day things that were occurring and her perspective on them. She expressed what the children meant to her and what I meant to her. I recall reading this over and over and crying an ocean of tears. This was one of the most cathartic things I did. I thank Geraldine for writing these beautiful words; she healed me from the Spirit world and assisted me through this process. I believe that on some level she purposely wrote these words for me to find after she was gone as she knew the end was near.

I have one other recollection of that time and I would like to share it with you. I saw on TV prior to Geraldine's passing away that Yusuf Islam (Cat Stevens) had just released a new album. I commented to her that we should get it to which she really didn't comment on.

I was in a shopping centre days after her funeral where I noticed the album and decided to buy it. I listened to this album on the way home. The first song was really nice, in fact, it was as if he never really left the music industry and this was just his next album. Just a classic song you would expect from him.

If I thought this was a good song the second song on the album took the word emotion to a whole new level. It sucked me in twisted me around wrenched all my tears out and left me feeling wonderfully cleansed. It was as though he wrote this song about and for her.

It expressed everything perfectly to the point that it made me feel as though her death was part of a bigger plan; she was expected to return home and I was meant to stay behind and finish something. Simply it made me feel as though someone had a grand plan that I didn't know and wasn't meant to for now.

I encourage you all to seek this one out and listen to it, it will touch you deeply. The Song is called "Thinking about You" by Yusuf Islam (Cat Stevens)

Outside of my immediate family it appeared that everyone had and I believe many of them are still having a very hard time coming to terms with the death of this beautiful person. I must leave them to process this passing in their own way and wish them the best on the journey they are taking for it is not an easy one. They will have many hurdles to overcome and I truly want them all to find peace with the world. I cannot do this for them as it is up to each individual to achieve their own peace. I can only say that there are choices in life that can be made and one must make them for their own betterment.

Spirit 7

The Grieving process is probably the most difficult and challenging part of the healing process, for it is here that people will generally come apart. I have some interesting insights to this subject that I would like to share, all are completely based on what makes sense to me and what worked for me during this process.

Grieving is about you not the person who has died. Grieving is a process for the people left behind, a rite of passage if you may, to help them get to the other side and find a way to continue their journey without their loved one. The most important thing is that it must have a beginning <u>and</u> an end. With an emphasis on an end.

One needs to remember that grief makes no difference to person who is gone, they are beyond this therefore it stands to reason that it must be for the people left behind.

I found myself not needing to think about it much, so I allowed the emotions to overwhelm me when they wanted to and I just let them sit there until they decided to pass. At least this way they were being processed.

I am not one to follow traditions, all the black clothes that people wear, visits to the graves and lighting of Angel Resin. To this I say do it if it helps you heal yet again I remind you that there are no obligations here - to anyone. This is your process to get through and no two people do it at the same pace or in the same way.

Another area that I have found people feel very driven during the grieving process is to do things the person used to do or to complete something the person had begun.

People will work extra hard, relentlessly in fact. They do this to complete things that the departed person used to do. I have observed people doing simple things like working to complete a vegetable patch, something their departed partner used to do even though it is exhausting for them. Maybe it is a way to maintain the connection to this person. If it helps do it but be sure that it is helping not hindering.

I myself went into overdrive, putting up many pictures that Geraldine never got to put up. They were probably not meant to go up; in fact there is a dent on a wall from one that kept on trying to fall out of my hands while trying to put it up. I really felt I needed to do it as that is what Geraldine wanted.....Or was it?

Upon reflection, I needed to put up the picture in order for me to be able to take it down again a month or two later. It was the process I had to go through. In my view Geraldine knew that the pictures were not meant to be up and she tried to knock them out of my hands yet like all Spirit she had to back off as it was not her journey any longer. It was mine and the final say is up to the person with the free will to make the choice. In fact I recall telling her to back off and let me go through my process. Remember my previous comment about the grieving process being about the people left behind not those who have departed. They will respect your choice.

During grieving some people don't heal because they are afraid to let the person go, they are afraid that they will lose this person who has died. They are afraid of dishonouring the person who has died. Same message again it is not about them it is about you, it is your process. I recall thinking the same thing many times, fortunately Geraldine usually responded with a kick up the backside to pull me back into line.

I recall one incidence where I was having a particularly bad day missing Geraldine and was in a very melancholic mood. I did as I always did when the emotions took hold, I allowed them to sit there and be processed. I would also put out to Spirit to tell me the cause of my anxiety. On this day, I found myself lying in the bath and the thought came to me that I will make a memory book for each of the kids. I will get photos of special moments and we can all write thoughts about the time. I would get the books printed up professionally and this would give a memento to the kids to remind them of their Mum when their memory fades. This will make Geraldine happy.

Immediately the thought came back, I couldn't care less, if I wasn't OK with their memories of me fading, I wouldn't have gone in the first place. At that moment I replied with "it will make ME feel better that I have given them something to ensure they can remember their Mum when memories fade" at that moment my anxiety and sadness left me...

Arrangements

One of the most overwhelming things to deal with was the funeral arrangements. After the vastly long time to process her death (two days) the funeral lady came over to assist me with organising the funeral (What fun I highly recommend it). Anyway, after two hours of choosing things for the funeral, I felt more drained than what I did after watching Geraldine die. At least it was done. She was going to be sent off in a white coffin, with white lilies on it as pure as her soul.

The day of her funeral I was strangely calm. I recall my kids asking me what they should wear. I said to them whatever they liked – there are no rules about this.

My daughter wore a flowery dress she bought with her mum and I helped my boys choose. They ended up wearing their Collingwood football jumpers. Their mum loved to watch them play footy and also barracked for Collingwood. This was a very special tribute to her.

The funeral itself and burial was a fairly typical sombre Greek occasion. I however shed very few tears, I don't really know why for sure. I do know that every time I looked at the coffin I would smile and think to myself how proud of her I was. She was an angel on earth and she had left this world. I would miss her counsel and company. I was however, so happy for her.

The other thing that stands out in my mind with respect to the funeral is a couple of people who turned up. I was standing to the side at the front of the church and had been kissed by about a million people (I remember thinking that I hoped no one had swine flu) when a man walks up to me and shakes my hand, I couldn't place him at first. As it turns out he was the builder who had built my house some 5 years earlier. Another person who turned up was the Architect who had assisted in designing the house. This was probably the best example of how this lady impacted all those people who came into contact with her. She simply had a way of captivating people, of endearing them to her and treating them with such grace and love that they almost felt indebted to her.

The rest of the day was unremarkable, a lot of pain and sadness. The person was sent off and we all went back to have a drink and remember the good times and begin the process of healing (at least that's what I did).

I would like to skip forward to the arrangement of her tomb for a moment and explain a couple of things. The tomb was selected by me as a tribute to this wonderful person. It has a lady draped over the side of the tombstone and a picture of Geraldine. Unsurprisingly the lyrics to the song mentioned earlier (Thinking about you) have been engraved on the ledger. And under her name on the tomb stone is a statement......

I was talking with the stone mason and he said to me that most people put "beloved wife of and mother of...." This just didn't feel right, I knew who she was and I said to him to let me get back to him with something.

About a day or so later my son, Daynon, was listening to songs at random on the computer. He played the song which has the Lyric that inspired the title of this book and is the statement under her name on the tombstone. The Song is called Oh very young by Cat Stevens. The Lyric is "Oh very young what will you leave us this time, You're only dancing on this earth for a short while" the hair on the back of my neck stood up. That's it! I thought "We're only dancing on this earth for a short while" perfect, it says it all. Every time people see it they can be reminded to live their lives, make peace and be happy. It is the essence of everything.

Life after death

This part of the story starts with an interesting Oxymoron - life after death; for life cannot exist after death. This is where the Spirit world exists.

This story is no longer about Geraldine for she is dead. It is about me who had to continue with my journey and leave Geraldine to begin hers anew.

The first month after her death was what could only be described as a blur of emotion. There were good days and bad, happy and sad but as indicated earlier I just let them happen. I refused to think about how I was going to deal with the future – that will come as it comes and I will deal with things one at a time.

This period was about dealing with the current emotion and doing exactly what I felt like at any given moment, be it with my children, friends or alone. The people around me at that time were wonderful and very supportive. However, I knew in the end I needed to face things on my own. They would all eventually go back to their lives so it was up to me to get through this.

I decided that the best form of defence was attack. I threw myself into the day to day stuff that needed to be done, things I could have been so easily forgiven for if I let them go.

On the day of her death my son had football practice and he asked me if he was going to go. I said to him "Son your mum said she wanted us to move on so yes you will go, moving on begins now". I was so glad I went; it was very strange standing there watching my son play football when his Mum had just died. Unbeknown to me at the time this was exactly what it was all about; getting some normality in our lives. Normality was something that we did not have for a very long time. And you know I think Geraldine was there watching with me.

I decided from that moment on that I was going to dive into every situation and be present. I took the kids to school and spoke to all who wanted to talk to me about Geraldine. I attended school functions – on my own. This was just my way of breaking free of it all, and the emotions well they would come and go; I let them.

Two things in this first month that really stood out for me were attending a wedding of Geraldine's cousin and doing a painting.

The painting that is on the back cover of this book is a painting I did in tribute to Geraldine. It is simply entitled "Geraldine". I had dabbled with oil paints for about a year and really enjoyed the place I went when I was in the zone and painting.

I had never done a portrait before. I thought if Geraldine could overcome all her fears, I could trust and give it a shot. I painted this portrait from a picture of her taken in happier times during a trip to Port Douglas. I recall the two areas that I spent particular time and care on were her eyes and her throat. The painting itself took two weeks to complete and is by many measures a very average painting, however it is from the heart and I believe really captured Geraldine's spirit.

The second thing in that month was the wedding. Some people were unsure if they should attend given Geraldine's death. At one stage I heard that the Bride wanted to call off the wedding. I called this person who I had never spoken to before (or at least I couldn't remember having done so) and said to her "please do not call off the wedding; you know that would be the one thing that would make

Geraldine frown down at you. You know her well enough to know that she wants you to go ahead with it, and I do too." I also said to her that I have every intention of attending the wedding.

I went to the wedding, I enjoyed the day and I even danced with the beautiful bride (WOO HOO). Yes I missed her yet that's no surprise, was Geraldine there? Absolutely she wouldn't have missed it for the world. When I danced with the bride I felt goose bumps and her caress, she was saying "well done."

The lovely couple took time out in their speeches to quite emotionally thank us personally for attending. This was just a re-affirmation that the right thing was done.

After the wedding I fulfilled a promise I had made to Geraldine about a year earlier, I gave up smoking. I took it up when she was re-diagnosed and promised that I would toss them out. I remember saying to her jokingly "babe I need a vice and you don't really need to live with a drunk right now" so smoking it was.

The following couple of months there was a lot of soul searching. Just working through the issues as they came up and trying to be there firstly for myself but also for my children.

Around this time my mind turned back to those healers that helped Geraldine so much. I decided to go and get a reading from one of them. I must admit that I was quite nervous. I had readings before but this was odd I just wanted her to come through but at the same time was accepting of the fact that she may not.

I went into the reading room and it was quite casual to begin with. There was a little activity and eventually she came through, how did I know it was her? Well the story that was expressed by the medium was something that had occurred between me and Geraldine and I know that nobody else knew about it, I never ever told anyone. I won't repeat it here as it is quite personal but those who know me know that they can ask and I would be happy to discuss it. Suffice to say it was obscure enough to leave me with my mouth ajar when the medium made comment about it.

There are things that I would like to note that occurred in this reading. One was that she came through in all her long haired glory; back to the person she was prior to being debilitated by this disease. I remember the medium saying I can see the person she was, the humour, her beauty and her charm, to which I replied "you see the person I fell in love with."

The second thing occurred right at the end of the reading; she thanked the medium for all he had done for her. This was her way; she never forgot anyone who helped her and she appreciated it.

To all of you that helped her cross over I would like to say thank you from the bottom of my heart, she actually took the time during the reading and made a point of saying thank you for making the transition so easy. This was done by all of you.

After the reading I got a business card from the school and decided the time was right to begin my journey of discovery of myself and the world through mediumship.

The path is one of discovery and learning but amazingly simple when it really comes down to it. If you trust and listen you can do it. It comes down to being committed to the cause and following the disciplines that get outlined.

My first Class was more of a long (very long) information session about what I was embarking on and some of the theory behind the things that were being taught. I will not discuss any of them as they are not relevant here. I can however recall that the more the man spoke the more it made sense and the more I wanted to learn.

I walked out of the class that night knowing that I was going to be back. The teacher asked me if I will be back to which I replied absolutely. I have been going ever since.

The following week I returned and was involved in the first class with the regular teacher.

The classes covered a lot of information about our auras and energy fields associated with our bodies. We were taught a number of things in these classes. Some of them I will share with you.

One aspect of this work was the concept of "shutting down". Some of you reading this will know what I am talking about for the others I will not go through the mechanics of what is done but the intention in very simple terms is to stop you from picking up on everyone else's crap and taking it on board. We were taught to do this process very often. After doing this for a while I must say a very interesting thing happened.

Up until the point in time that I started shutting down I thought I had gotten my emotions under control. This was correct, to a certain extent I had come a long way and believed I had gotten the emotional side of me under control. I was really like a closed champagne bottle, under control as long as the lid stays on. However, if the lid pops off (as they all do eventually) they result in an explosion. Once I started following the disciplines of shutting down I found an amazing sense of balance (I actually remember talking with a friend and saying I feel emotionally like I did about 5 years earlier when things were very normal in my life). This is the point when I realised just how powerful the tools being taught were.

Other areas that have been amazingly beneficial include Meditation and the healings. Those interested can ask me about them and I'll be happy to do my best to answer.

A few strange things have happened to me since I have begun the newest chapter in my life. I would like to share some of them with you.

Readings – It has been a fascinating experience doing readings for people and class members. Some were face to face during class and others are done absently outside of class and passed on to the students in class. It has to be one of the best feelings when people indicate that they can place the reading. One of the best experiences was when Geraldine actually came through and had a message for someone around the area of health. That person was very lucky to get a reading delivered from her.

I recall getting the image of Geraldine when I was doing the reading and I thought to myself this can't be happening. I sat there and fought it for a minute, she just sat there looking at me in the end crossing her arms and fixing me with a look that could only have been hers. Finally in my mind I thought *"it is you isn't it?"* She raised an eyebrow nodded. I then said (or thought rather) *you have something to say don't you?* She replied with a look that said *about time stupid* as well as a nod of confirmation. We did the reading and it was wonderful to communicate with her and deliver such wonderful information.

There have been some other smaller things that have occurred like my daughter having misplaced a piece of amethyst somewhere and not knowing where it was. She asked me "have you seen my Amethyst?" I immediately heard a voice in my head say outside, and before I realised, I said to her "have you left it outside?" She remembered where she had left it and went straight outside to get it.

There are many stories like this that I could repeat yet they are all similar. There is one more I would like to share as it was a particularly strong one.

I Have been seeing a Kinesiologist regularly through to the end of 2010 and as needed beyond that. I attribute a large amount of my initial ability to overcome what has happened in my life to the sessions I had with this man. He would bring up stuff that I didn't know existed so they could be dealt with. It worked amazingly well although there were times when it was exhausting.

Six months after Geraldine's death I decided to take my kids to him to ensure they were coping. The result was interesting. He indicated that my daughter appeared to be having some emotions that were sitting on her lungs. Interestingly, I was just talking to her a few days earlier and she was complaining about not being able to take deep breaths. After the session this issue was gone. The two boys both seemed pretty good apart from some expected emotions of sadness and anger.

I have decided to take the children regularly to assist them to clear any emotions they are bottling up. Anyway the real reason for telling you all this was to tell you what happened on the way home.

I was driving home and I got a sudden very emotional feeling in my solar plexus, I started to cry. I remember thinking what on earth is going on? Where did this come from and realised pretty quickly that it wasn't mine.

I put a thought out there, *whose is this*? Shortly after saw the image of Geraldine to my right and above. She was clasping her hands in front of her near her chest and she was crying tears of pride. She told me how proud she was of us all for doing what we just did. She then gave me a message for each of her children. To Caitlin she said "stop wearing the cloak of motherhood, you are going to be a wonderful mother one day but it is not your time right now" I repeated this to Caitlin and I asked her if she could place it and she said yes. To Geordie she said "It is OK to be angry with me, I'm a little angry with me too." He didn't say much but I know that it hit home because he looked as though someone had exposed a secret.

To Daynon she simply said "I am proud of you for opening up the way you did".

At this point I really wanted to talk more but I was driving so I said to her "babe thanks for coming through but I need to stop this now; I can hardly drive and talk at the best of times let alone do this. Please come again to me at another time I would love to talk further." With this she left having given me the most wonderful experience. I recall thinking *how can I miss her too much when she pops in like she does?* I truly have been blessed to have her say hello every now and then.

I have also done a Reiki healing course. The thing that struck me the most about the course was how simple the whole thing was to do. Once I was attuned to the Reiki and Seichem Master level I felt an amazing calm come over me. The feeling was incredible. I found myself feeling quite able to approach topics that I would never have had the ability to approach prior. Only because I seemed all of a sudden able to deflect or ignore peoples negative reaction and still be able to deliver a message that needed to be delivered.

The conversation I had with my sister in law on the night after the first day of the course about some people's health and my concerns would never have occurred had I not done the Reiki course. I would have been fearful of a reaction and irritated at the denial that ordinarily came with these sorts of discussions. However this time I just needed to express my concern and for the first time I couldn't care less about the reactions that may or may not have come back.

This was one of the first times I stopped caring what other people think. This is one of the most valuable things I have learnt to now and still find very important the less you care about what others think and say about you, the happier you are.

Since then I have done a number of healings on myself and others. The healings are helping people and this is wonderful. It is something that I will continue to do and help whoever I can with this and other healing modalities.

The other outlet I have found of incredible benefit has been painting. If what I experience through the process of painting is similar to other artists then we should all be a little envious of them for they have a true and real way to be in touch with Spirit.

Painting is the most amazing outlet. I have found that the process of creating the image in your mind and applying the image to a canvas is something that has left me breathless. I find myself at times coming up with images or names of a title in my head.

Usually the title is the way I get the information first. I will go and write it down on my list of titles along with any ideas that may be in my head associated with the title. What usually happens from there is the title remains there until the universe gives me inspiration to read the list of titles again.

As I am reading them one will capture my attention and I will know what I need to paint. I know the feeling as it is the same feeling you have when the person you care for smiles at you. Your heart just knows that something has fallen into place in a major cataclysmic way. In fact, you know that if you can't paint the image the way you saw it at that moment you are not meant to do the painting and you will need to move on to something else.

Let me tell you about the experience of a painting that at the time of writing this I had not yet started. Four months earlier I had seen a painting of a lady smelling a flower and I got the idea to do something similar of a lady blowing a kiss.

The decision to paint this particular painting was finalised when a friend asked me what I was going to paint next.

I was finishing a painting that I had started prior to my wife's death some 6 months earlier. I never thought I was going to be able to complete it as it was representative of a previous time (or so I thought).

Funnily enough, I had decided recently to finish it and I was comfortable inside (truly comfortable) with the decision to finish it. Is it any surprise that shortly after this decision was made I also started to date again and further more is it any surprise that this painting was called New Beginnings by me many months earlier? At the time I thought it was for a different new beginning. I believe Spirit knew better? Anyway I digress.

As we were talking, I had the very strong urge to show them the list of paintings that were to be done after this one. I was reading down the list telling the person what they were about and how I felt about them. I was actually saying about all of them that I was not ready to paint them. As I said it about this particular one I choked up and started to cough. You see in my view Spirit didn't agree with me on this and didn't let me say that I wasn't ready so I put the question to them.

After asking my friend to wait a minute and staring blankly at nothing according to them (I didn't recall doing that). I actually got the title of the painting "Poseidon's Daughter" and I knew exactly how the painting was meant to look; a graceful lady blowing a kiss with the ocean behind and the calming blue of the sea as a theme.

To explain this when you connect with your guides and Spirit they will use many ways to get a message through to you. In this instance I was avoiding working on the painting or finalising what it should be, I was procrastinating. They stopped me talking to make it clear that it was ready to be painted.

The image of a Lady in a beautiful purple-blue dress blowing a kiss came to my mind and I turned back to my friend and said to them. "I will paint this one next; it is going to be a caricature style painting of a lady blowing a kiss." Funnily enough, this time I was able to say it without choking up making me aware that it was correct.

It was one of those moments such that if the painting cannot be painted this way it was not to be painted at all. Since then I have found myself staring into space imagining the perfect form for the body and how to capture the beauty in her face. My spirit guides help me with this as I find they feed me a lot of the images that I need to make the painting work. The challenge is to get into the zone where you can do the images justice in the real world (let alone the ability to make them come to life).

Since that time, I sketched the image I wanted to use. As per every time, I do my paintings there is a transformation from the original idea to the final design of the image to be painted.

The experience of painting for me is very strange. Once the canvas is touched by the brush the world stops for me. I am working in a zone where understanding what colours need to go where and how to shade things seem to simply make sense. I look at the painting as though I am part of the paint and simply one brush stroke changing one millimetre of the painting makes it look completely different. I find myself later struggling to remember why I made some changes only that they worked for me.

The inspiration to paint usually comes after I put the intent out that I want to paint a particular section next. I find that usually a couple of days later I would be driven (sometimes at very strange hours) to do the painting. The other scenario is when I link the intent to paint some part at a particular time or location. I find that I have to do it no matter what and the painting gets done quickly and easily – far faster than I could ever imagine.

So life after death definitely exists for those who are left behind, they just need to re-engage themselves after someone's death. Those who have died are still around you, just give them permission and they will help. This however, is your choice – to live your life. No longer should you play the victim, blaming someone who has died for not being able to move on. Moving on is your responsibility – yours alone.

Lastly I have penned a response to the beautiful poem Geraldine wrote....

These are my words to you Geraldine:

BIRD WHO FLEW

Watched you grow
Became the person you must be
Your will casting all doubt aside
Beautiful bird, wings flying wide
Soaring in the sky, Journey ended
Yet a new one begun
Honoured I am to have played a small part

As you fly away I look back in time
Smiling at the person you were
At a time where a smile eased my weary heart
At a time where holding of hands was healing

I see you at times, feel your caress
Comfort me still as you know who I am
Your loving embrace still always missed
Your charm and your grace always, amiss

Alas, it is what it is
I wish it not to change
For most grateful am I
To have had true loves embrace
The greatest gift of all was mine.

Thank you

There are many people that have assisted me on this journey. Every single one of them has made me who I am. I will single out some people for a personal thank you below, yet I wish to say a few things to all of you that have helped me on my journey.

Some of you have taught me to live again, through this I have found myself again. I have found the strength to walk on my own and trust in what I know to be correct; to really stand in my truth. You have made an impression on me that cannot ever be changed, no matter what life brings you have all impacted my heart. I don't need to name you as you know exactly who you are.

Some of you have taught me to reflect upon myself and stop blaming others for issues that are being caused in my life. You have taught me not to take other people's issues on board and leave them with their issues. I have grown so much through the teachings and am forever indebted to you for the guidance.

So now to some specific people I wish to thank...

Geraldine

To you I say simply thank you. Thank you for choosing me for your journey, thank you for showing me love. Thank you for setting me on the path that I am on. Thank you for being who you are and allowing me to help you. Thank you for my children, thank you for your grace, thank you for making me a better person, thank you for allowing me to carry you when you truly needed it and telling me to step back when you needed your space. Most of all thank you for coming back and communicating with me and the children. I can only strive to make you proud.... We will always love you Babe.

My Children

Caitlin, Daynon and Geordie. To you I say you have been my little earthing rods, always grounding me when I get ahead of myself and helping me grow when I was down. Your simple beauty and pleasure sustains me and reminds me of the beauty of everyday life. Through you I will always have happiness and pleasure. You are all amazing and know this: <u>You have played a huge part in helping your dad get through a difficult time and for this your dad will be forever grateful and in your debt.</u> You are more than my children you are people I am proud to call my friends.

Anna and George

Anna, you are one of the few people on the face of the earth that showed me no judgement while I went through my own journey. You have shown me great patience, crying with me in my sorrow, laughing with me in my happiness and healing me through my pain. You have given me strength in my moments of weakness, slowed me down when I was rushing and kicked me in the pants when I deserved it.

George, you have shown me great patience and always have been there to make me laugh even when I was hurting and dying inside. You have no matter how much I didn't like it always told me how you saw it and for this I am grateful. You have been very important in keeping me sane throughout the whole process I have been through.

I am blessed to have people in my life as special as both of you. So I will say to you both simply thank you, you are a true friends.

Brett and Dawn

To my mentors and teachers. To both of you I can only say you have stood by me through thick and thin and helped me learn more than I could ever imagine. You are more than friends you are family.

Irene

You have come into my life and shown me true unconditional love again. You have validated that I am on the right path because you choose to walk it with me. You love me for who I am and you inspire me. You are my council, my rock and the love of my life; evidence that if you choose to heal true love will find you again. Thank you for being in and part of my crazy little world. I love you very much.

Final Thoughts

What would you do if you knew you could talk with someone who had departed? Just imagine it for a minute what would you ask? Now just close your eyes and believe it, ask the question out to them; you may be surprised at the result.

Geraldine made peace by dealing with the emotional baggage that was hurting her; this is why she was able to move on to the Spirit world in peace.

The most important thing I learnt while watching Geraldine go through her journey was when pain or grief comes your way do not move to lessen it. Embrace it, delve into it, befriend it and allow it to consume you; you will be surprised how quickly it will pass leaving you cleansed. Hold on to it or hide from it and it will be presented to you again, at another time possibly through illness.

Remember that whatever issues you need to deal with are your own. It does not matter how trivial they seem to others, what matters is they impact you. The greatest power comes from understanding that for whatever reason the issues are indeed impacting you and that you must deal with them. The brave will deal with them and come to be at peace with them. This is the way to allow your soul to heal and progress in its journey.

One of the hardest of all issues to deal with is grieving. Remember to allow the grieving to occur, move to hide from it and it will simply become one of those issues that you will need to deal with at some stage. The key is to remember it is about you, not the person who is gone. They are beyond it and care not if you grieve or not, they just want you to be happy. You must remember they cannot make this happen only you can.

One thing I would like to say is how many times you hear that I wish I had said this or that after someone has died - TOO LATE! You need to accept this as a lesson and ensure it does not happen to any other person in your life. The dead have moved on and you need to forgive yourself for anything you may have done wrong to them or how you may have let them down. Remember there were many good things you did as well so you need to accept your errors and move on. Only you are holding on to the errors and regrets they have moved into a realm of healing and learning and have unburdened themselves of the negative energy. Remember the option to talk to the person is there – take it.

To those who think a lot of the things I do and believe are a bunch of crap, to you I say this: I could have been forgiven for becoming an alcoholic, a manic depressive or even if I ended up on the streets shutting myself off from the world (believe me I know how easy this would have been to simply not feel). Instead I chose to sit in my pain, embrace it, process it and come out the other side a better person. This was achieved by me through determination and hard work for part of the journey. It was completed and lifted to a whole new level by the skills taught to me in Mediumship.

There are many who disagree with Mediumship. To them I wish them well on their journey yet I have In-sourced my spirituality, deciding to take responsibility for my own path instead of leaving it to others. I have learnt to work on my flaws and be the best person I can be – can you all say the same for yourselves?

Remember seeing isn't believing, believing is seeing – do not make the mistake of getting it the wrong way around.

Finally I say to you all I hope you have gotten something out of this book; it took a lot for me to write it. Please remember not to judge what people do and only treat them the way you wish to be treated, for this is the true reflection of who you are.

Oh, by the way, I decided to swallow the bitter pill that was presented to me this time....

Epilogue

I wrote the most part of this book leading into Christmas of 2009. As I reflect on the year I find myself thinking about the gut-wrenching lows that have occurred. Then I find myself thinking about how they have been dealt with and the incredible highs that have also occurred.

Since that time I have developed my skills as a Medium and as a healer. I have seen much change in me. The experience of love again and loss again has all been there. The overwhelming sense is that I am my own master and happiness can only come to me from me. If people wish to share my happiness I welcome them if they don't that is their decision. I however, move forward in love and light and stand in the light of the truth of who I am. The one constant that has always been there is Spirit.

I feel incredibly lucky in my life – I always thought I was lucky in life to find love once and to know I found it again is just the most amazing feeling of appreciation that it leaves me breathless. I have five beautiful Children who I am so proud of and I also feel pretty proud of myself as well.

Remember all of you; it is easy to feel sorry for yourself only the brave choose the journey of happiness.......

Life's good.....

THE BEGINING

Reflections of the Medium

Although this book was written through the second half of 2009 it has taken a long time for me to come to terms with it and be ready to publish it. I have finally reached this point and just when I finished re-reading the book in 2015 a voice came to my head and said so what was the beginning like?

The beginning, my journey, what do you do when all has been stripped away from you? Where do you go when you have nothing left? What is it you are meant to be doing when your soul has been stripped bare and everything has been torn away from you and then thrown back at you for good measure? What are you meant to be doing? What do you do? Well that bit is easy, you take a step and then another and keep on doing this even if you have to fake it to begin with until things start to improve

I have decided to add this section to complete the book. The completion is my journey into the afterlife, that is, the life after Geraldine. As indeed reflecting back now it does seem that both of us died that day and both were re-born anew. The only difference is I got to do it in a physical existence and she got to go home.

I have done much thinking and developing in this time. I have learnt much in the short time after Geraldine's death.

One of the first things that struck me as I reflected upon this time was how do you get over something like this? How do you move on? Well firstly let me clarify something, you never get over something like this, it always hurts and you always remember. So this notion of getting over something, meaning that you forget and move on is rubbish. You learn not to let it impact your future life, that is all; don't expect the pain to go away. If the pain remains it is as it should be.

I can tell you what realization I had that makes me believe I have gotten over Geraldine's Death. I recall with only happiness when I think back about her or when memories pop into my head. For example: the memory of the beautiful lady walking down the aisle, there is only happiness there, not even a twinge of sadness, only happiness for a wonderful memory.

If you recall the happy memories as just happy memories, then you really are in the realm beyond grief. This is where the death of someone will not haunt you and you are free to be – to simply just be.

To reach the place of just being requires you to deal with your issues and needs you to be brutally honest with yourself as there is no worse person to lie to than yourself. Be kind to yourself as most people do not reach this space easily and the ones who do only do so with hard work and with significant amount of effort.

Self

OK right here I could ramble about many things yet I have found that the key to success is self. This does not mean you need to be by yourself, only that you need to be honest with yourself. Be honest enough to:

- See how far you have come and be proud of the effort you have put in.
- Acknowledge what is still to be fixed
- Accept love and happiness when it presents even if you do not feel ready, after all when are you truly ready?
- Be ready to accept that the self does not get lost unless you allow them to.

For me in truth, the things that set me free were the realisation and acknowledgement that I was OK with Geraldine's death. It was sad yet no matter what anyone else's judgement was I had moved on and entered a new phase of my life. The other thing that gave me a paradigm shift was I am not here to fix anyone else. I am here to fix my own soul and that is enough work in itself. I will help where I can yet that is the limit and key only where I can.

So when it comes to self be the best you can be. Don't focus on past mistakes we all make them and likely will again. Remember if you want to be good at something you need to exercise the skill. Believe you me; walking the path of self-truth is one that requires you to be constantly battling with your human nature. Your soul's nature is the one you need to tap into…

Me

Well what has happened with me after all this time? I am working as a medium full time. I have found that it is the most content I have been in my life. I have experienced relationships on many different levels in this time. Each one of them has taught me a valuable lesson about, you guessed it, myself. Finally when I least expected it, I have had the love of my life come into my life. I can honestly say if you open your heart and accept the lessons (and hurt) that come with doing this, you will find what you seek. Yes dreams do come true I am now married and have a beautiful blended family of five Children and the most beautiful lady in the world.

The secret is contentment with self-love and true love with another. Contentment will allow you to be and true love will inspire you to be all you can be.

Ultimately, love is giving up some of your power and vulnerability to someone else. True love is when the person you offer your vulnerability to returns it and says thank you I don't need it, why don't you have mine instead?

This is why true love is hard to achieve. You essentially must face your fear because you are giving someone the power to hurt you and in return they must also choose to face their fear and do the same in return.

Validation

I firmly believe everyone has some form of intuition. If we all listened we would all receive messages.

I have spent a number of years now giving readings and healings to people. I truly believe that I am helping people with their lives and am giving them an understanding of the current path they are travelling.

I think the most powerful thing is bringing through people's relatives to them to give them some sort of closure.

I have brought through many different relatives for people from a distant grandparent to children who have crossed to remind the ones left behind that they really haven't been truly left behind at all. All of my readings and connections have been special and I find no greater happiness than when I reconnect people to their crossed loved ones.

It needs to be said that a relative will not come through every time you want them to. It is not an exact science and generally as a minimum it can take 3-6 months before they are able to come through. I have even had a case where someone was waiting 8 years and they still hadn't received a connection.

However, when they do need to get a message to you they will. I don't normally share details of a reading yet I will share this one as it was done in a public platform event and it really explains how Spirit can manipulate things to get a message through if they really need to.

I was at a festival and normally there are workshops throughout the day. I regularly do proof of life where I try to connect with people's crossed over relatives. Each person gets a half hour workshop and on this day a colleague and I decided that we would do both of our sessions together.

We did the first slot and it went fine. When it came to the second slot I had gotten bookings for private readings, I couldn't go. I recall the workshop started at 3 and I was waiting for my client to come. At about 3:10 I kept on hearing in my head go to the workshop continuously. I eventually relented and I went to the workshop expecting that my client was a no show.

When I got there I couldn't believe what I saw the lady who was coming to me for a reading had one of her relatives come through and my colleague was giving her information, no wonder she didn't show up!

I decided to do my part since I was there and connected to an entity. There were two ladies sitting one behind the other with an empty row in between them. The spirit being was standing in the empty row between them. Neither could place all the information that was coming through. Eventually a lady to the right sitting in the same row as the spirit was standing said she could place the information.

I asked her can you place the stomach cramps and bloating she said her partner had passed from Crones disease, how about the personality I described? Yes that was him and the month of July is relevant to him? Yes it is month he was born in. OK we are with you…..

Information came through about him and all of a sudden I looked at the lady and I said "he is saying to me he is going to dance at your wedding." She burst into tears. She had a new partner and was thinking about getting married and was wondering if he was OK with it.

She came up to me afterwards and gave me a hug and said the weird thing is you actually look a bit like him so it was like him telling me.

I was so grateful to be able to give peace to both of them. If you consider the effort this person in spirit went to from distracting my client and ensuring she was getting a reading and bugging me to go to the workshop. Finally connecting to give the information to his loved one so she could move on it is amazing. It reminds me if we pay attention they will get the information through. They will work hard for us if we are willing to be open and listen.

Final Word

Before I go I wish to leave you with something I discuss regularly in my workshops. It really is an attempt to get an understanding of what it all means.

We all have heard the term "unconditional love." Especially people in the spiritual field say this all the time. Now me being me, I thought about this term and said to myself *what is this thing unconditional Love?* Now I know we can look at the meaning of the words and try and understand through that yet how does it feel; how do you know it?

After a number of days contemplating I received a message, "who is a being of unconditional love?" In my head pops an image of Jesus, not the religious icon, the man. After researching him a little I found out his Galactic name is Sananda. Now when Sananda was being hurt and persecuted he was still a being of love. I thought about him; I found myself realising that here was a man that could understand other people and give them love even though they would eventually kill him. Mind you he was capable of also being hard on people when he needed to be.

So unconditional love does not equate to softness, it actually equates to understanding others and being able to give love and wish people well even when they are trying to hurt you. This equates closely to empathy; the ability to understand and put yourself in another's position even though they may be hurting you.

So again, me being me, I went a step further and I thought, well how do we become empathetic? Through experience came the answer. And then the penny dropped: experience can only come through lessons…. Hence the reason for all these blasted lessons we get over many lifetimes!!

In truth, we are all on the same path as the great ascended masters like Sananda, Budda and others. In order to get there we have to become beings of pure empathy, beings of unconditional love. Then the lessons will no longer be required and we will be able to progress to the next level of evolvement. So embrace your lessons and do the best you can, maybe we can shift things and become what we were all destined to become…….Perfection.

The New Beginning

For more information about the author, Leonidas Kolokathis visit www.emeraldhands.com

Acknowledgements

Many people have encouraged and given feedback for this book, you have all encouraged me to put this in writing and get it out into the world, I thank you all.

Terry Goodkind:

I first picked up The Wizard's first rule and quickly realised I was not going to be able to put it down. It was more than a great story it was inspirational in the way it made the reader reflect on life. Since then I have read all the books in the Sword of Truth series and each and every one has had a profound way of making me reflect on myself. Terry you truly have a gift, thank you for the stories that assisted me in my darkest hours.

Quotes used in this book have come from the following Terry Gookind books:

"Life is in the future not in the Past" – Pillars Of Creation, Terry Goodkind 2001

"Your Life is your own – rise up and live it" – Faith of the Fallen, Terry Goodkind 2000

"In the middle of the journey of our life I came to myself within a dark wood where the straight way was lost"

And

"The path to paradise begins in hell"

Are from Dante's Inferno.

Printed in the United States
By Bookmasters